BRITISH LORRIES IN COLOUR

S. W. Stevens-Stratten

First published 1994

ISBN 0 7110 2245 3

© Ian Allan Ltd 1994

Designed by Richard Souper

Published by Ian Allan Publishing

an imprint of Ian Allan Ltd, Terminal House, Station Approach, Shepperton, Surrey TW17 8AS; and printed by Ian Allan Printing Ltd, Coombelands House, Coombelands Lane, Addlestone, Surrey KT15 1HY.

IAN ALLAN
Publishing

Front cover
1947 Austin Model K4 Lorry
A K4 5ton long wheelbase lorry which spent its working life on general haulage duties for a mill at Nailsworth in Gloucestershire. It is seen here at Puton Stoke, near Swindon, in October 1992. Peter Durham

Back cover
1955 Commer Dropside Lorry
This 1955 Commer Dropside lorry, fitted with the TS3 two-stroke diesel engine, was owned by Weston's Cider of Much Marcle, Herefordshire. It is pictured here at Fonthill Bishop in Wiltshire. Peter Durham

Above
Ford 2ton Dropside Lorry
This 1956 Ford 2ton Dropside Lorry is outside Weston's Garage and Service Depot. The garage and depot were built in 1926 for Weston's, the Cider and Perry Makers, of Much Marcle in Herefordshire. The garage still retains its prewar splendour with attended pump service at the 1937 petrol pumps. Peter Durham

INTRODUCTION

The dictionary definition of the word 'heyday' is ...'The period of greatest popularity, success, fashion, power or the like; the prime'. The heyday of the British lorry, therefore, depends from whose angle you are viewing the subject. From the operators' point of view it could be from the early 1960s when Dr Beeching closed so many railway lines that practically everything had to be transported by road, even though a few years later the British commercial vehicle industry was in almost terminal decline and the choice of vehicles severely limited, with foreign manufacturers coming to the fore. From the enthusiast's point of view this was a retrograde step and for him the heyday was probably just prewar when the variety and types of vehicles on the road were at their highest, with no MOT restrictions and plenty of aged lorries to be seen — even though some of them may have been mechanically suspect by today's standards.

By the mid-1920s the transport of goods by road was becoming established; pneumatic tyres, windscreens and an enclosed cab were becoming standard. In the early 1930s Scammell of Watford pioneered the articulated vehicle while multi-wheeled rigid lorries were becoming more common with an increase in the payload capacity. Diesel engine development had reached the stage where they were reliable, economical and were being offered as an option by many manufacturers; in fact ERF and Foden never supplied a petrol-engined vehicle.

Prewar there were approximately 33 different British companies producing commercial vehicles — today there are only three which are British-owned. It is fortunate that this position did not exist when World War 2 commenced, for the British commercial vehicle industry had a proud record for the production of many thousand of lorries for the War Department, the Ministry of War Transport

and concerns engaged on priority war work, plus the production of tanks and munitions.

As a result of the 1947 Transport Act many famous road haulage concerns were nationalised. This led to a loss of the individual companies' identities and the trend towards standardised fleets. It was much later, with contract/lease arrangements and the privatisation of the remaining nationalised elements of the industry, that the roads of Britain became more colourful.

In the 1950s forward-control was the normal configuration and even the light and mid-weight mass produced models turned away from the bonneted vehicle, and articulation became more popular, especially on trunk operations.

It must be remembered that in 1948 the law restricted vehicles of over 3ton unladen weight to a maximum speed of 20mph, and the maximum weight was 15ton — apart from special vehicles carrying abnormal loads.

By the 1960s technical advances were rapidly made with turbo-charged engines, air-operated disc brakes and suspensions, pre-selector or automatic transmission and lifting tailboards — to name but a few.

The design of bodywork has dramatically changed since the 1920s. Cabs are now more streamlined and fitted with heaters, radio, and even a sleeping compartment at the rear. Although the flatbed or platform lorry is still extensively used, curtain-sided bodies have, to a large extent, replaced the tarpaulin-sheeted and roped loads. Hydraulic ram tippers and grab-loaders have eliminated the driver and his mate wielding a shovel! Aluminium and reinforced glass-fibre panelling is now used in place of wood and steel for cabs and bodywork.

Such is the march of progress, but the old vehicles are part of our heritage and examples must be preserved in the same way as works of art and other artefacts. We cannot praise too highly the dedication and skill of

the preservationists who restore these old vehicles which are often found as a derelict wreck and are brought back to original and pristine condition. Many are not skilled tradesmen, yet they spend years of their spare time working on their project in an old shed or barn — often in their back-garden! We must also pay tribute to the work of the Historical Commercial Vehicle Society who cater for the enthusiast of commercial vehicles over 25 years of age. They offer advice, issue a magazine, and organise rallies which show the history and development of the transport scene over the last 70 years or more.

It is unfortunate that colour photography was not really developed until the mid-1950s so colour photographs of early vehicles actually working are virtually non-existent. All the vehicles portrayed in this book have been preserved.

1917 AEC Y Type

The Associated Equipment Co (AEC) built, in its original Walthamstow factory, more than 10,000 of its Y type lorries for the British army between 1916 and 1918. The company installed what is believed to have been the first moving track production line in Europe and completed vehicles were rolling off this line at the rate of one every 30min. Fitted with a four-cylinder 45hp petrol engine and four-speed and reverse crash gearbox, the strong chassis of the Y type could carry loads far in excess of the WD rating of three to four tons.

After the cessation of hostilities many of the surplus ex-War Department vehicles were sold in the civilian market, and AEC continued to produce this model, with variations in wheelbase and other details, until 1921. Many haulage concerns commenced business with these vehicles as the backbone of their fleet and many lasted well into the 1930s. By that time many had been fitted with pneumatic tyres.

The 1917 example shown here is at the conclusion of the HCVS's London-Brighton Run in 1992. It was sold in 1924 to Beedon's of Northampton, who converted it into a charabanc and fitted pneumatic tyres. It was found in the 1960s and restored by Sparshatt's, the commercial and bus bodybuilders of Portsmouth. It is now owned by Brian Gibson in Sussex. Peter Durham

1936 AEC Mammoth Major

Introduced in February 1934 the AEC Mammoth eight-wheeler for up to 14¹/2 ton payloads, was a logical development of the four and six-wheel range of chassis. The model became extremely popular and was originally fitted with either a six-cylinder overhead valve petrol engine or a six-cylinder AEC oil engine. The overall length was 27ft 7in and the wheelbase 16ft 10¹/2 in, although a shorter version was also available. The Mammoth Major continued

in production until the outbreak of war in 1939. In 1947 the Mammoth Major was again featured in the AEC range, but with modifications. It was then fitted with the 9.6 litre six-cylinder oil engine developing 125bhp. The new wrap-round cab was fitted on models from 1958 onwards, and this was succeeded by the Ergonomic cab in 1964, with again increased engine size and variations in wheelbase.

Widely used by the heavy haulage industry, it was fitted with a variety of bodies, including both

tipper and tanker variations. The type was the mainstay in the fleet of a great number of concerns including London Brick Co, Parks of Portsmouth, British Road Services, Pickfords, Shell-Mex, etc. The 1936 AEC Mammoth Major shown here is owned by Lloyds of Ludlow who have several preserved vehicles. The photograph was taken in a period setting in Ludlow. Peter Durham

1946 AEC Monarch

The early postwar Monarch Mk III range was for a gross weight of 12ton which meant a payload of approximately 7¹/₂ ton. Basically the same as the prewar model, the newer version was fitted with the well-known 7.7 litre oil engine and the rear axle used roller bearings instead of the plain ones used previously. With vehicles in short supply following the war years, the Monarch was extremely popular

with a vast number of road haulage firms of every description.

This platform lorry, with a suitably sheeted load, was supplied new by Oswald Tillotson to its first owner Brooks Concrete of Halifax. It was found in a poor state and restored by its present owner and is seen here on the HCVS's Trans-Pennine Run in 1993. Peter Durham

1936 AEC Mammoth Major — 6

There were only 10 of these vehicles built in 1936. They were unusual as they were normal-control or bonneted lorries. They were also lightweight and the saving can be seen in the rear axle which has only a single tyre.

Nine of the 10 vehicles built were in the fleet of J.O. Lyons & Co for the transporting of tea and confectionery. This particular vehicle was sold to a showman in 1949 who operated it until 1968 when it was again sold. It then had two owners before purchase in 1990 for restoration. It is now fitted with a Gardner 5LW oil engine. It was photographed at the HCVS's Trans-Pennine Rally in 1991. D. A. Reed

1962 AEC Mercury Lorry

The AEC Mercury was redesigned and a completely new model appeared in 1953 with the new 'rounded' cab. It was designed to carry an 8ton payload. At first it was fitted with a choice of 6.75 litre diesel giving 98bhp or the famous 7.7 litre diesel of 112bhp. Later the Ergonomic cab was fitted and there was also a wider choice of available engines. The chassis was uprated for 10ton loads from 1955.

The example illustrated here was first registered in May 1962, a few months before the tragic news that AEC was being acquired by the Leyland organisation. The London Brick Co was among a great many hauliers who operated the AEC Mercury chassis with a variety of bodies. It is seen at the Birmingham Outer Circle Rally in September 1990. Jonathan Webb

1965 AEC Mandator Mk V

The name Mandator was used by AEC as far back as 1931 for a 5ton chassis, in either normal or forward (cab-over-engine) control. In 1935 the payload was increased to 7½ ton. A completely new model was introduced in 1956 with the, then, modern wrap-round cab and apart from the four-wheel rigid version, the short wheelbase (9ft 6in) model became very popular as a 32ton tractor unit for use with semi-trailers.

Mandators were used by many firms and the tractor units were seen all over the country hauling semi-trailers carrying a wide variety of loads.

This vehicle was new to Munro's of Aberdeen and, after many years of trunk service, it was used as a yard 'shunter' until 1982.

It is seen here coupled to a four-in-line trailer at the AEC Rally at Wollaton Park, Nottingham in May 1993. Peter Durham

1936 Albion KL127

The K range was introduced in 1935 for a payload of 4^1/$_2$-5^1/$_2$ ton. The standard wheelbase was 12ft, but a shorter version at 10ft 9in was designated KS and the longer one of 14ft was the KL model. All were supplied with the Albion four-cylinder petrol engine rated at 22.5hp. The K series remained in production until 1942.

These lorries were widely used for medium requirements, and could be seen with operators all over the British Isles.

This vehicle was new to Ernest of Eccles. It was driven by its current owner from 1946 to 1968 when he purchased the lorry and placed it in storage. It was fully restored by C&G Coachworks of Much Wenlock. It was photographed at Ditton Priors, Shropshire in October 1991. Peter Durham

Above

1948 Albion Model CX7

The CX range was first introduced in 1937 and the first eight-wheeler of the new models appeared a year later. The engine was later increased in power to a six-cylinder 120bhp unit. The wheelbase was 18ft 3in and these vehicles could carry a payload of 18ton. There were no outward changes in design between the pre and postwar models.

These vehicles were popular on trunk routes with many operators and Bulwark Transport had a large number in its fleet of tankers.

This preserved example is seen in Harrogate on the HCVS's Trans-Pennine Run in August 1993. D. A. Reed

Right

1937 Albion Model P557

Produced from 1935 to 1938, the model P557 was available in three different wheelbase lengths (13ft to 16ft). The short one was designated PS557 and the longest one PL557 and all were designed for a 6ton payload. A choice of six-cylinder engines was available — 43.4hp or 48.6hp. Vacuum servo-assist ed brakes operated on all four wheels.

The P557 was operated by many companies engaged in road haulage throughout the UK carrying the widest variety of goods.

This 1937 model was new to E. A. Majors, a general haulage contractor of Highbridge in Somerset, and used mainly on its trunk services. It was restored by a previous owner in 1977 in the livery of his own company. It was purchased by Maurice White of Warrington in 1992, and has been rallied regularly by its new owner. The photograph was taken at Malpas Rally in September 1988. Denise Plum

Above
1947 Austin Model K4 Lorry
The similarity between the 2/3ton K2 and the 5ton K4 can be seen at a glance. Under the bonnet the similarity also existed as the same six-cylinder 27hp petrol engine was fitted.

The K4 5ton long wheelbase dropside lorry depicted here spent its working life on general haulage based at a mill in Nailsworth, Gloucestershire. It was restored in 1991 and is seen in a country lane at Purton near Swindon in October 1992. Peter Durham

Right
1926 Bean Flatbed Lorry
Bean commercial vehicles were made in Tipton, Staffordshire from the early 1920s until 1931 when the company went into liquidation. The heaviest chassis the company produced was for a 50cwt load, but the lighter vehicles were car-derived. They were popular with the retail trade for a short time, as they were competitively priced.

This 1926 Bean was exported to Australia, hence the non-original cab. It was later brought back to the UK and is now displayed at the Black Country

Museum, Dudley, close to where the company was based. Peter Durham

1936 Bedford Model WLG Cattle Truck

Bedford, part of the American General Motors Corporation, began life in Britain as Chevrolet but, in 1931, the range was completely redesigned and produced under the name Bedford. The company soon adopted the slogan 'You See Them Everywhere' which was very true for the vehicles were a reliable first class product for carrying capacities from 15cwt to 5ton and, being mass-produced, they were sold at a very competitive price, with easily obtained and economical spares.

Bedford continued to use the company's six-cylinder petrol engine of 27.3hp in its range for a number of years.

The WLG model was for a 2ton payload and the standard wheelbase was 13ft 1in. This vehicle was originally acquired for carrying livestock for a business in Sevenoaks, but later worked in the Isle of Wight. It is seen here on the HCVS's London-Brighton Run in 1992. Peter Durham

1942 Bedford Model OWST

During World War 2 Bedford made over 250,000 vehicles for the armed services. In 1941 the company was able to produce a civilian version of the OY military model which was designated OW. It was designed to carry a 5ton payload and all models — three wheelbases were offered — were fitted with the well-proven six-cylinder 27.3hp petrol engine. A four-speed crash gearbox was also standard as were Lockheed servo-assisted brakes on all four wheels. All the wartime models can be distinguished by the austerity 'square' bonnet and radia-tor grille. The vehicle illustrated here served with the RAF on airfield construction work and was then sold to an operator in Devon, where it was first registered in 1960. It has been restored by its current owner, Ron Minchin. Peter Durham

Left
1947 Bedford O Type

The Bedford O type was introduced in the late summer of 1939, so very few appeared prior to the war. The range, with its 13 variations, was marketed immediately following the cessation of hostilities and continued in production until 1953. The type was extremely popular with all users for they were reliable, economical, the cost was within reason and both spares and servicing were readily obtainable.

Originally fitted with a cattle wagon body, this example of a Bedford O type was found derelict on a farm. It was restored by its current owner and photographed at Park Farm, Ettington, in June 1993. *Peter Durham*

Above
1949 Bedford O Type

This is the OLBC 5ton model of 1949 fitted with a convertible cattle truck body by Vincents of Reading. It was originally purchased as a chasis and cab. It was used by its original farmer/owner until purchased for preservation in 1991 and subsequently restored.

It was photographed at Longcot in Wiltshire. *Peter Durham*

Above
1956 Bedford S Type Lorry
Bedford introduced the S type in 1950 for 7ton payloads. The Bedford S was the first of the 'Big
Bedfords' which were to follow. With semi-forward-
control and differing wheelbases plus a short wheelbase 8ton tractor unit, the S type soon had a
foothold in the commercial market. At first only
a petrol-engined model was available, but very
soon the choice of a diesel engine was offered.

The 16ft flatbed lorry seen here at Elvington in
July 1992 originally carried a body for the Auxiliary
Fire Service. D. A. Reed

Right
1928 Chevrolet Lorry
Chevrolet vehicles were imported from the USA in
knocked down form for assembly at Hendon,
London, during the 1920s. Owned by General
Motors, the vehicles were the forerunner of the

Bedford trucks. The LP range had a four-cylinder
21.7hp engine and could carry a load of up to
25cwt. The cost of the chassis in 1928 was £190.
Chevrolets were not, however, sold in the same
numbers as similar capacity Ford vehicles.

This particular lorry was supplied to a coal merchant in Ludlow, Shropshire who used it for a number of years before selling it to a farmer who left it
to decay in 1942. It has now been restored to its
original condition. It was photographed in the
evening sun at Ashwood Bank in September 1992.
Peter Durham

Amgueddfa Diwydiant a Môr Cymru
HOWARD'S
HOWARD'S TRAVELLING STORES
HIGH CLASS GROCERIES & PROVISIONS
SERVICE AND QUALITY
TX 8259

Far Left
1929 Chevrolet Model LQ Van

The LQ model was similar to the LP but fitted with a six-cylinder 26.3hp engine and the payload was 30cwt.

This mobile shop has a body purpose-built for Mr Winston Howard of Wenvoe, Cardiff, for his business selling groceries and dairy produce to remote villages around the Vale of Glamorgan. It was photographed outside the Welsh Industrial Museum at Cardiff in June 1991. Stephen Hansford

Left
1931-32 Commer Truck

Commer Cars was among the earliest of commercial vehicle manufacturers and had set up an impressive production line and range of models by the early 1930s. Never becoming a threat to the really heavy vehicles, Commers nevertheless excelled in the 2-4ton class.

The Raider illustrated here is typical of the era. It was powered by a 22.6hp Commer six-cylinder petrol engine and had a carrying capacity of 30cwt. T. Brown

1958 Commer QX Dropside Tipper Lorry

In the late 1950s and early 1960s Commer powered many of its vehicles with the company's revolutionary TS3 diesel engine which had a capacity of 3,261cc. This was a two-stroke engine with three horizontally opposed cylinders, developing 105bhp.

The style of cab and radiator grille is typical of Commer products of this period.

This vehicle worked until 1987 on a farm. D. A. Reed

1971 Commer Maxiload Lorry

Although badged as a Commer this is a Dodge design, for the latter concern took over Commer in 1964 and a year or so later the company was gradually integrating the Commer range into its own. This model still retained the Rootes TS3 two-stroke diesel engine. G. Dowling

1934 Dennis Ace

In 1934 Dennis produced its first Ace model; this was soon to be known as the 'Flying Pig' due to its protruding bonnet. These vehicles proved popular for light/medium loads as the payload was 2¹/₂ ton and they were supplied with a four-cylinder petrol engine which developed 242.8hp. The short wheelbase of 9ft 6in gave a tight turning circle and thus they were useful for urban work. Several parcels delivery firms had the Ace in their fleets, and they were also popular with municipal authorities as refuse collection vehicles and gully emptiers.

The example shown here is entirely original and seen at Harrogate at the end of the HCVS's Run from Manchester in 1992. D. A. Reed

1958 Dennis Pax

Pax was the name given to Dennis's prewar 5ton lorry. The design remained unaltered until the late 1950s, which shows how modern it was, for its time, when it first appeared. It was available with petrol or oil engine.

It is strange, but Dennis-made vehicles seem to have been popular with the brewing industry as it operated large numbers of differing models over the years.

Note the 'boxes' over the back wheels, necessary for the low platform which made for easy loading. It was photographed in appropriate surroundings at the Whitbread Hop Farm at Beltring, Kent.
R. Matthews

Above
1946 Dodge Lorry

This was a popular prewar Kew-built design of an American truck manufacturer. The cab style had been introduced in 1936 and was common to all models. Dodge short-wheelbase chassis were often used with tipper bodies. In 1939 it became possible to fit some of the larger carrying capacity chassis with a Perkins diesel engine.

The 5ton 101B shown here is typical of the Dodge designs of the period. It served its original owners, Shorthall Bros of Stone, until 1956 and covered over 300,000 miles. D. A. Reed

Right
1954 Dodge 7/8ton Tipper

The Dodge range changed its outward appearance in the early 1950s by using a similar cab to those

used with Fords and Leyland Comets. The payload range was also increased by adding a 7ton version, which was often used by sand and quarry merchants with a tipping body.

This tipper is fitted with a five-speed gearbox and a two-speed rear axle. It was seen at the Upton-upon-Severn Steam Rally in June 1991. Peter Durham

Below
1959 Dodge Lorry

An entirely new range was introduced in 1956-57 with normal control, an option of a Perkins engine and yet another cab design from Motor Panels which was also used on Leyland and Albion badged vehicles — hence the name LAD cab (Leyland, Albion, Dodge). This is a 3145 model for a 7ton payload with a wheelbase of 13ft 7³/₈ in, and was one of the last models to be produced at the Kew works of Dodge.

This preserved lorry was originally a petrol tanker and was last used as such in 1968. It has now been converted to a dropside lorry and is seen here at the 1992 HCVS's Trans-Pennine run at Harrogate. D. A. Reed

Right
1936 ERF Eight-wheeler

The initials ERF stand for Edwin Richard Foden, who broke away from the family concern in 1933 and began manufacturing diesel lorries. The company soon became one of the leading manufacturers for operators found that ERF produced a rugged, no 'frills' and reliable vehicle. The range extended from 6ton four-wheelers to eight-wheelers which were to appear in 1936. All models were fitted with Gardner engines, four-speed crash gearboxes, single-plate clutch and overhead worm rear axles.

They were soon used by many of the major trunk operators in the UK.

This example has had extensive restoration and was seen at the CVRTC Classic Commercial Show in June 1991. G. Dowling

1946 ERF Type LK44 Model 5ton

The ERF 5ton lorry is the smallest the company produced and was first manufactured in 1935 with Gardner 4LK diesel engine of 53hp and four-speed gearbox as standard. With a choice of three different wheelbases the model continued in production until 1955, but it was redesignated LK44 in 1946 when a five-speed gearbox was fitted. In 1954 an Eaton two-speed rear axle was fitted.

This example was originally owned by Ushers Brewery of Trowbridge and was sold in 1972. However, the company repurchased the lorry for preservation in 1976 and restored it to the original livery. It was seen at the 1991 Bristol Festival of Transport. Simon Chapman

1959 ERF Model 56GTS/KV

In 1952 ERF completely redesigned its cabs and radiator grille adopting the oval grille that distinguished the company's products from every other make. This oval design was common on all the KV models and lasted until 1961 when another new cab was introduced. These models were used in all branches of road transport.

This vehicle was new to Humphreys of Watford. It was seen at Harrogate on the HCVS's Trans-Pennine Run in 1991. D. A. Reed

1962 ERF Series LK44G Van

It is not so common to see a van body on an ERF chassis, but this attractive body was built for Benson Toffees of Bury. The van was an exhibit at the 1962 Commercial Motor Show at Earl's Court, London.

It is seen here at the 1993 HCVS Trans-Pennine Run having been restored in a new livery.
Peter Durham

1966 ERF LV/A Series Lorry

Over the years ERF has become the leading British manufacturer; in fact in 1993 it was the only British owned maker of heavy commercial vehicles — apart from Dennis which specialises in fire appliances, municipal vehicles and buses. The LV series was introduced in 1962 with a range from 6ton to 42ton and a wide variety of wheelbase options. Engines could be Gardner, Perkins, Rolls-Royce or Cummins. The cab is a glass-fibre product on earlier models but, from 1972, a Motor Panels steel cab, similar to those on Guy, Scammell and Seddon, was fitted. From 1970 the models were redesignated the A series.

This model is now with its third owner, but was new to a market gardener in Newent, Gloucestershire, then sold to a coal merchant in Gloucester and now forms part of the new owner's haulage fleet. It was specially positioned at Sharpness Docks for our photographer. Peter Durham

1926 Foden Steam Wagon

The days of the steam wagon ended in the late 1930s although many were kept running during the war. The coming of the diesel engine, which is always ready to run at a moment's notice, needs no stops for water, is not the subject of restrictive legislation and can be operated by one person, made operators realise that steam traction had its limitations. In their heyday steam lorries were popular with many large fleet owners, particularly in the brewery trade.

Of the two best known makes — Foden and Sentinel — the example shown here is typical of the former manufacturer. It is a 6ton dropside wagon used new by Edward B. Devenish of Rayleigh, Essex, on a contract for the London & North Eastern Railway carrying manure to market gardeners in the area. It then had two further owners before seeing service as a tar sprayer on road works. In 1959 it was again sold, this time for quarry work at Harmby, North Yorkshire.

It has now been preserved and is seen here passing St Leonard's Church in Brighton near the end of the HCVS's Run in 1990. A. Swain

1955 Foden Lorry

Foden commenced manufacturing diesel lorries in 1933. These were fitted with Gardner engines and soon became popular. Eventually a range covering all payloads from 6ton upwards was built. Foden diesel lorries were soon in the fleets of many large operators including the Cement Marketing Board, various brewers, and many long-distance haulage contractors.

This 1933 S type is typical of the early models fitted with a straight radiator. It was supplied new to the West Norfolk Farmers Manure Chemical Co-operative of King's Lynn. It has now been preserved and is seen here in Kidderminster in 1989.
Mike Matthews

Below
1954 Foden FG6/15 Lorry

In the 1950s Foden was at the forefront of heavy lorry manufacture. The products of the period were distinguished by the postwar redesigned cab and radiator grille. Large numbers of this type were sold for all classes of heavy work.

This vehicle was new to Eye Haulage and is typical of many used by transport contractors. It was later operated by Turners of Soham and later saw service with Wilsons, the showmen, of Redditch. It has now been restored to its original condition and is seen here at the Classic Commercial Show in 1991. G. Dowling

Right
1959 Foden S20 Flatbed

Possibly a natural progression from the cab style of the FG was this 'rounded' design for the S20 which was known as the 'Sputnik' cab or 'Mickey Mouse' cab. For payloads of up to 16ton on four wheels this type proved to be an economical vehicle, and it was used in all spheres of road transport.

New to E. & O. Cooke of Bourne, Lincolnshire, the S20 illustrated was used for carrying potatoes to markets throughout the country. It was stored in a barn for 10 years with a broken half-shaft before being purchased for preservation in 1989. It has subsequently been restored and was photographed at the CVRTC Classic Commercial Motor Show near Rugby in 1991. G. Dowling

1963 Foden Eight-wheeler

This Foden eight-wheeler is now in the hands of a contractor in the amusement business. It is typical of so many heavy haulage vehicles which are able to enjoy further service hauling loads of Dodgems, Swirls and other such rides. They are also used as tractor units, often with a generator over the rear wheels and pulling a trailer.

This example, judging by its short wheelbase, probably carried a cement mixer body when it was first registered. A. E. Peacock

1925 Ford Model T Van

The famous Ford model T, often referred to as the 'Tin Lizzie', was first produced in 1908 in the USA and assembly in Britain started in 1911. Designed to carry a load of up to $7^1/2$ cwt this was often exceeded. They had a four-cylinder 22.4hp engine with a two-speed epicyclic gearbox. Often the butt of music hall jokes, the model T was to see the commencement of many haulage businesses in the 1920s. On ascending very steep hills when fully loaded (or overloaded) it was not unusual for a model T to go up backwards! This was because the reverse gear was a lower ratio than the first gear.

There were many thousand model Ts built from 1911 until production ceased in 1927. A heavier model to carry a payload of 1ton was the model TT which was of similar outward appearance, apart from a longer wheelbase.

This preserved model is often seen at rallies. G. Holtom

1929 Ford Model A Truck

The model A followed the model T in 1927 and had a payload capacity of 10-15cwt. Supplied with a four-cylinder side valve engine developing 24.02hp, it had a three-speed gearbox.

Until production finished in 1934 to make way for the model B these vehicles were popular with the retail traders.

This preserved example is seen in the HCVS's Bournemouth-Bath Rally in 1992. Peter Durham

1935 Ford Model 51 Lorry

In 1935 Ford adopted a totally different shape for the radiators of the company's 3ton 51 models, not unlike its Y type cars but with the addition of two horizontal bars. Fitted with a 30hp V8 engine they were quite fast vehicles for their time. The standard wheelbase was 10ft 11in. The model had a relatively short production life for the series finished at the end of 1936, when it was succeeded by the 61 series.

A variety of bodies were fitted to this chassis, but it was not extensively used by the large haulage concerns.

It was photographed at Harrogate on the HCVS's Trans-Pennine Run in 1992. D. A. Reed

Below
1947 Ford Model 7V
The Ford model 7V was a forward-control chassis for carrying a load of up to 5ton. By this time Ford were offering a choice of engine — a side valve of 3,285cc or a V8 of 3,622cc capacity. A choice of four wheelbase versions was also available. The 7V proved to be a reliable and tough vehicle and it remained in production until 1949, and during the war many emergency fire tenders and heavy units were built on this chassis.

This preserved 5ton, three-way tip lorry was new to Tarmac Ltd at their Corby Depot, and has been returned to that company's livery. It is seen in 1992 on a Dorset Historic Road Run. Peter Durham

Right
1961 Ford Thames Trader Dropside Lorry
The Ford Thames Trader forward-control chassis was introduced c1958 and remained in production until 1966. It was a large range with payload capacities from three to seven tons and short-wheelbase tractive units for hauling semi-trailers. The vehicles all had the same cab design, although there were small variations on the grille and headlamp panels, and no other manufacturer had a similar cab style. A normal-control Thames Trader was not so popular as the forward-control version which could be seen on many retail distribution jobs and used by smaller business organisations. Some tipper bodies were fitted to the short wheelbase 5ton and 7ton models, but they were so often overloaded by cowboy operators that their reliability suffered.

This preserved model was seen at the Great Dorset Steam Fair in September 1992. Peter Durham

1934 Guy Wolf Lorry

Designed more for the retail trade and the lighter side of haulage, the Guy Wolf was introduced in 1933 for a payload of up to 3 ton. It was available as a normal-control or forward-control vehicle. Both had a wheelbase of 12ft 6in, although a 10ft 6in wheelbase vehicle was also available from 1936. Originally powered by a Meadows petrol engine of 20.1hp, in later years a Perkins P4 diesel engine could also be fitted.

The Wolf models were fitted with a wide variety of bodies and, although not produced during the war years, the model was revised in 1946 and remained in production until 1959.

This Wolf was photographed at the Wincanton Steam and Country Fair in July 1993. *Peter Durham*

1949 Guy Otter Tip Lorry

Guy moved into the heavier market in 1937 when they introduced the Otter 5/6ton chassis, which weighed only 2$\frac{1}{2}$ ton fully equipped. Again, using either a Meadows petrol engine or a diesel engine, the model, with a wheelbase of 12ft 7$\frac{3}{4}$in, remained unaltered up to the outbreak of war in 1939 when production ceased. A revised model appeared after the war with a choice of three different wheelbases with a more modern look to the cab. The Otter was popular with many medium-haul operators.

This model, fitted with Meadows petrol engine, has Pilot underfloor tipping gear and spent its working life around Stoke-on-Trent carrying foundry waste. It was photographed in a country lane near Hay-on-Wye, Herefordshire in August 1992. *Peter Durham*

1966 Guy Warrior Articulated Van

This was one of the last type by the company before Guy Motors were finally absorbed into the Leyland organisation. Rigid and tractor units were manufactured, which could be fitted with engines from AEC, Meadows, Cummins or Rolls-Royce. The artic vans were essentially for the long-distance trunk opera-tor, and many famous firms had Guy Warriors in their fleets.

This typical example, owned by Cavewood Transport, was used on TIR work and made regular journeys to the Paris area until 1972 when it was sent to Germany as a shunter. It was repatriated to England and is now used for special occasions. This particular vehicle has a Leyland 400 engine and a six-speed gearbox with a two-speed rear axle.
A. E. Peacock

1965 Guy Invincible Tipper

At the 1958 Commercial Vehicle Show great interest was shown in the new Guy Invincible model, which was exhibited at the show. Available as a six or eight-wheeler with three differing wheelbases, the type was originally fitted with a six-cylinder Gardner diesel engine, but later many other engines could be fitted — Cummins being one of the most popular.

These Guy products had moderate success in the commercial vehicle field, but faced stiff competition from other British makes. Competition was also faced from some of the continental manufacturers who, at this time, were starting to gain a foothold in the British market.

The vehicle illustrated here was new to Pioneer Cement and was still working for its living in 1990. It is seen at the Guy Owners Rally at Wolverhampton Racecourse in April 1990. Denise Plum

1977 Guy Big J4 Tractor Unit

Guy Motors introduced the Big J range of vehicles in 1964, after the takeover by Jaguar Cars and just before that group of companies was absorbed into the Leyland organisation at the end of 1964. Production of Guy vehicles continued until 1978 when it finally ceased. The Big J range used the Motor Panels cab as fitted to Seddon vehicles at that time. The Cummins turbo-charged six-cylinder diesel engine developing 146bhp was the standard power unit, and the range included rigid four, six and eight-wheelers as well as four-wheel tractor units.

The Big J series was used by quarry owners and trunk operators as well as heavy haulage contractors.

The tractor unit shown here was seen at the Guy Owners Rally at Wolverhampton Racecourse in 1990.
Denise Plum

Above
1969 Karrier Bantam Platform Lorry
The Karrier Bantam started production in 1934 after Karrier's had been taken over by the Rootes Group. It was updated in 1948 and again in 1963. Over the years it has been popular as its small diameter wheels and low chassis have made it ideal for use as a light rigid low-loader for a load of up to 2 ton. It has often been used by municipal authorities for refuse collecting work.

This platform lorry was seen at the HCVS Tyne-Tees Rally in 1992. D. A. Reed

Right
1924 Leyland Type A1 Lorry
The Leyland model A was first produced in 1920 to carry a load of two tons. A four-cylinder 25.5hp engine was fitted with a four-speed gearbox and a worm drive rear axle. A year later the engine size was increased to 32.2hp and then, in 1922, the carrying capacity was increased to 2^1/$_2$ ton. Many of these old lorries gave yeoman service, being later fitted with pneumatic tyres in later life. The A1 series remained in production until 1926.

This platform lorry was new to Birtwell's of

Blackburn and later saw service with Hine Bros of Shaftesbury in Dorset. It has now been preserved and is seen here on a summer evening during August 1993 at Gillingham in Dorset. Peter Durham

1934 Leyland Badger Lorry

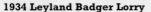

Leyland started to name its various products from 1928 and the Badger was allocated to the 2¹/₂ ton TA series. It originally had a 25.6hp four-cylinder engine and was offered with three different wheel-base lengths. In 1932 the engine power was increased to 28.9hp and the payload increased to four tons. In 1935 a 30.8hp diesel engine was offered as an alternative. Although not the most popular of the Leyland range in the 1930s, the type was none-the-less used by many large concerns.

This 1934 Badger sided lorry, fitted with a canvas tilt, was shown at the Upton-upon-Severn Rally in July 1992. Peter Durham

1940 Leyland Lynx Lorry

The Leyland Lynx was produced by Leyland in the late 1930s as the answer to meet the competition from the mass produced vehicles in the 5ton payload range. Given a six-cylinder 29.4hp petrol or diesel engine, it was available in three wheelbase lengths — 12ft, 14ft or as a tractor or tipper at 10ft 3in. The Lynx was a nice looking vehicle and was gaining in popularity when production ceased soon after the outbreak of war.

The model depicted here was used by the War Department and, on being released at the end of hostilities, was operated by Askham Bryan Agricultural College at York. It was later transferred to the Ministry of Agriculture at Silsoe.
P. J. Chancellor

1948 Leyland Beaver

The Beaver range was first produced in 1933 for 7½ ton payloads. Over the years both normal and forward-control models have been produced, but the former was dropped after the war. There have been a wide range of payload capacities, wheelbases and engine sizes as the Beaver was well-liked by all branches of the road haulage industry.

This platform lorry — carrying a van-type body common to many hundreds of the type — has had a varied career. This includes acting as a mobile X-ray unit and as a builders lorry at Bath University. It is now restored as a general haulage lorry and it was photographed in August 1993 in a Mendip lane. Peter Durham

1950 Leyland Octopus Lorry

The Octopus was the name Leyland gave to their 15ton eight-wheeler when it first appeared in 1935. At that time it had a six-cylinder engine and was available with either a 16ft 10in or 18ft 10in wheelbase. Like the Beaver, Octopus production has continued over the years (with the exception of the 1939-1945 period) and there have been many variations. Thus the last vehicles to be built bore little resemblance to the original 1930s model.

The Octopus has been used extensively by long-distance hauliers and, when British Road Services was formed, the new company placed a large order. This vehicle worked from various BRS depots in the London area until transferred to Sheffield depot in 1960. It was purchased by a showman in 1962 who used it until 1981. It has now been restored to its original condition. G. Dowling

1948 Leyland Comet 75 Platform Trailer

One of the first of the new postwar range of vehicles produced by Leyland was the Comet model, which was a semi-forward-control chassis for 6ton payloads. It was distinguished by a completely new front-end design, which was unlike any other Leyland design. In 1952 another version — the 90 — was introduced for 7$\frac{1}{2}$ ton loads. Two years later forward-control models were produced using the

LAD cab. The Comet models remained in production until 1960 and were used by all types of commercial vehicle operators.

This lorry is in the livery of the well-known Lincolnshire produce merchants, Walter Smith, who ran several Comets delivering potatoes to Lancashire and Yorkshire and to collect seeds and other agricultural produce. Now preserved, the Comet is seen at Elvington in July 1992. D. A. Reed

1949 Maudslay Meritor

The Maudslay Motor Co was formed in 1903 and produced cars and light vans. The company later progressed to commercial vehicles up to a 5ton payload and, during World War 1, produced some 3ton army lorries. A range of heavy goods vehicles was produced from 1921. However, sales were never in the 'top ten' and the company had many financial traumas. In 1939 a completely new range was announced but production did not begin in earnest until after 1945. In 1946 the company was taken over by AEC, although it continued with the new design thereafter with an ever-increasing level of AEC parts included. The Meritor was the name given to the company's 15ton eight-wheeler. The type had only limited success within the transport industry as it faced fierce competition from a range of other manufacturers.

This example of the Maudslay Meritor is seen in Nottingham in 1984. D. V. Page

1949 Morris Commercial Type CV11 Lorry

Morris produced its CV22 models in 1937 with two versions to carry 30cwt or 2ton. Both models had a 11ft 6in wheelbase and were powered by a Morris 24.8hp four-cylinder petrol engine. The payload was increased to 3/3$\frac{1}{2}$ ton after the war, although production of the CV11 range ceased in 1950.

The CV11 models were in direct competition with Bedford and, after the war, with Austin. The vehicles were used mainly in the retail distribution trade.

This particular lorry was used on a fruit farm near Tewkesbury to take produce to the railway station and local retailers. It is seen at the CVRTC Commercial Show, near Rugby, in May 1992. Paul Chancellor

1936 Scammell Rigid Six

The early 1930s saw the introduction of the Scammell Rigid Six with a carrying capacity of 12ton. Powered by a four-cylinder 85hp petrol engine it had a 19ft wheelbase and was fitted with 13.5 by 20 tyres — singles on the rear bogies. Being an economical vehicle with a comparatively light weight, the Scammells became a regular sight on the trunk roads of the British Isles. The model was produced as a flatbed and with sided and van bodies.

This example, originally owned by A. E. Dawson of Leighton Buzzard, is seen at Harrogate in 1992.
D. A. Reed

1938 Scammell Articulated Tanker

Scammell Lorries of Watford was among the pioneers of articulated vehicles, a type of vehicle which is now taken for granted on the roads of the late 20th century. When introduced, however, the type did not receive universal acclaim amongst the operators. Despite this, many petrol companies started using Scammell tractor units coupled to frameless welded tankers. These tankers could carry up to 3,000gal of fuel. Similar trailers could also be used for the transporting of milk and other liquid products.

This particular vehicle was delivered originally to W. H. Cowburn & Cowpar of Trafford Park, Manchester, and completed some 1,260,000 miles in use before withdrawal in 1972.

This survivor of the earliest days of articulated road haulage is seen at the CVRTC Rally in 1991. G. Dowling

1946 Scammell 45ton Ballast Tractor

Scammell has always been at the forefront of heavy traction by manufacturing a range of heavy ballast tractors of varying sizes capable of pulling low-loader trailers carrying weighty loads. Scammell produced two 100ton tractors during the 1930s. The outward design remained unaltered during the 1930s and this example is the penultimate chain-driven tractor which the company produced.

Although completed in 1946, the company retained its prewar design.

This tractor unit worked for a showman until 1972, when it was purchased for preservation. It is seen hauling a representative load at the CVRTC Rally in 1991. A. E. Peacock

1947 Scammell Rigid Eight Van

The Scammell Rigid Six was immediately followed by the Rigid Eight. This was a forward-control model launched in 1937 for handling 15/16ton loads. It was supplied with a Gardner 6LW diesel engine as standard and fitted with a six-speed gearbox and epicyclic rear axle. Considered as a fast mover in its day, the design remained unaltered until the early 1950s. The type could be seen on all the main trunk routes in the country and was used extensively by long-haul operators such as Young's Express, Fisher Renwick, Whitbread's Brewery and many others. The Rigid Eights were given the nickname of 'Showboats'.

This 1947 model was new to Young's Express of Paisley and passed to British Road Services on nationalisation in 1948. It has now been restored to its original livery. Robert V. Tuck

1948 Scammell Rigid Eight

Similar to the previous photograph, this illustration shows the Rigid Eight as a dropside lorry which was originally owned by Fisher Renwick before passing to Young's Express. It was also taken over by BRS in 1948 and the newly nationalised concern allocated it to the company's Southampton depot. It was later moved to Canterbury where its body was changed for London market duties. P. Chancellor

1942 Scammell 15LA and 20LA Tractive Units

Scammell tractor units have always been extremely popular with showmen and a great many have worked out their final days on fairground work as they are powerful and therefore ideal for pulling heavy drawbar trailers. With this work a generator was often fitted over the 'fifth wheel' where the coupling for the semi-trailer was located. Many of the articulated tractor units used originally by the petrol companies have subsequently been used by showmen and many carry names traditionally associated with the showmen's earlier steam lorries.

Pictured on the A303 near Andover en route for the Salisbury Charter Fair in October 1991 is this 1942 Scammell. Used by R. J. Rawlings Amusements of Ashford, the tractor has been christened Pride of the South. Peter Durham

1947 Scammell 6ton Mechanical Horse

Much has been written about the mechanical horse. This was originally introduced in 1933 to replace the horse for use on local deliveries. The mechanical horse drew a semi-trailer, which was often a converted horse cart. Two models were produced — the MH3 for 3ton payloads and the MH6 for 6ton payloads. The four-cylinder engine developed 14.5hp. Production of the MH6 continued until 1946 when it was succeeded by the Scarab model. There was little external difference between the 3ton and 6ton models and the styling varied little during the lives of both designs. Both the MH3 and MH6s were used extensively by all of the 'Big Four' railway companies and by many other local delivery operators on parcels services. Graham Etchell

1961 Scammell Scarab Mechanical Horse

The Scarab was introduced in 1948 to replace the MH3 and MH6 models, one of which is illustrated in the previous photograph. The concept remained the same, but notice how the design had been modernised. The 6ton version now had a 45bhp engine (at 3,200rpm) while the 3ton model was fitted with a 25bhp engine. The combined engine, gearbox and rear-axle unit was located behind the cab.

This example of the Scarab, seen in the livery of J. T. Watson of Dewsbury, is pictured at Barnsley in July 1992. D. A. Reed

1948 Seddon 6ton Lorry

Seddon produced its first vehicle in 1937 when a chassis for a 6ton payload with a chassis weight of only 50cwt was put on the market. Powered by a Perkins six-cylinder diesel engine, the model was just establishing itself when the war intervened. The model reappeared at the end of hostilities and the range was expanded in the following years. The original model found favour with many hauliers as the chassis was lightweight and, as a result, it was economical to operate and could legally travel at 30mph.

The vehicle shown here, seen on the HCVS Tyne-Tees Rally in 1989, was new to T. Silcock & Sons in 1948 and remained in regular use until 1980 for the carrying of farm produce. A. E. Peacock

1957 Seddon 3ton Lorry

One of the first vehicles in the company's new range appeared in 1950 when the Mk 7 model was introduced to handle a 3ton load. Again it was powered by a Perkins engine, but this time of a four-cylinder type. Although used by a number of concerns in the retail distribution business, the type did not have a great impact on road transport.

This preserved example, dating from 1957, is seen in Leicester in May 1991. Peter Durham

1925 Sentinel Super Steam Wagon

Two names dominated the steam era in road haulage terms: Foden and Sentinel. The Sentinel 5/6ton standard, first manufactured in 1906, and the smaller 4ton standard of 1914 both had vertical water-tube boilers, solid tyres and chain drive. The success of these vehicles was such that they remained in production until 1923 when the Super

Sentinel was announced. The new Super model also had the vertical water-tube boiler, but had double chain drive to the rear axle. Vacuum brakes could also be fitted at an additional cost. In 1931 pneumatic tyres and steam braking could be fitted as optional extras. Three different wheelbases were available. Production continued until 1932, when the DG models, introduced in 1926, became the main range available.

This 1925 Super dropside wagon was new to Leopold Walford Transport of Manchester. Later the Sentinel company fitted it with pneumatic tyres and it was sold to Puddifors of Birkenhead. It finally passed to James Grains, who used it until 1950. Now preserved, it is seen passing St Leonard's Church, Brighton, in May 1990. A. Swain

1934 Sentinel S4 Steam Wagon

Further advances were made in steam wagon design in 1933 with the first appearance of the Sentinel model S4. This model saw the appearance of steam-assisted brakes on all wheels and the final drive was through a double-reduction rear axle. The usual vertical water-tube boiler was employed feeding a four-cylinder poppet valve engine. It is unfortunate that restrictive legislation stifled the progress of the steam wagon and the last S4 was produced in 1938. However, in its five years of production, a large number of S4s were sold for general haulage.

Photographed at a rally at Bishop's Castle in August 1992, this steam wagon was delivered new to the Cowlairs Co-operative Society in Glasgow for transporting coal and coke. In 1956 it was relegated to tar spraying with Durham County Council, but it has subsequently been restored to its original livery. D. A. Reed

1955 Sentinel Type DV44 Diesel Lorry

Sentinel entered the diesel-engined market in 1946 as steam wagon production had all but ceased. The last steam wagons were produced in 1949 to complete an export order to Argentina. The DV8 was a forward-control 7/8ton vehicle with a Sentinel-Ricardo horizontal four-cylinder engine of 36hp. With a modern looking cab, it was available in two wheelbase lengths — 12ft 6in or 13ft 4in. A few six-wheelers for 10ton loads were also produced. In 1957 production ceased and Sentinel was acquired by Transport Vehicles (Warrington) Ltd who used up the stock of chassis and parts, fitting them with the Commer two-stroke engine.

This particular vehicle spent its working life with Booths, the steel stockholders of Bolton. It has now been preserved and is seen here at the Robin Hood Inn at Castlemorton, Worcestershire,

1929 Star Flyer 3/4ton Lorry

The Star Motor Co was never in the mainstream of commercial vehicle manufacturers and throughout its existence from 1904 (as the Star Engineering Co) to its final demise the company had a traumatic existence, largely as a result of financial problems. They were taken over by Guy Motors in 1927 and continued as a separate entity until going into liquidation in 1931. The Star Flyer was the company's most successful model. Living up to its name, the Flyer was a fast vehicle for a 3/4ton payload and was powered by a six-cylinder 23.8hp engine.

This particular example was photographed at Lydbury North in August 1992. D. A. Reed

Far Left
1918 Thornycroft X Type 3 1/2 ton Lorry

Following the J Type, which was a 'subsidy' model for World War 1 and which was so successful that it remained in production until 1927, Thornycroft produced the X Type in 1918. Designed to carry a payload of 3 1/2 ton, it had cast-steel spoked wheels and the brakes acted on the transmission as well as the rear wheels. It was powered by a four-cylinder engine developing 32.4hp. It was photographed at the Bishop's Castle Rally in August 1992. D. A. Reed

Left
1919 Thornycroft J Type Lorry

The Thornycroft J Type was a 'subsidy' model produced for World War 1 and many thousands were built. Such was the success of the model that production continued up until 1927, although many changes and improvements were made during this long production run. Throughout, however, the lorry remained designed for a 4ton payload. The original engine fitted was a side-valve four-cylinder petrol engine developing 32.4hp, with a four-speed sliding pinion gearbox. In 1924 this engine was replaced by one giving 36.1hp.

Apart from new models off the production line, many ex-War Department vehicles were also put on sale after the war and many ex-servicemen started transport businesses with one of these lorries. Many firms big and small were running J Type Thornycrofts well into the late 1930s.

This particular vehicle is now preserved by its original owners, Wethereds Brewery of Marlow. K. Marshall

Below Left
1927 Thornycroft Model A2 Lorry

Making its first appearance in 1926, the Thornycroft A2 was a popular vehicle for payloads of 2 ton. It was powered by a Thornycroft four-cylinder petrol engine rated at 22.5hp. The same engine also powered the A1 model. The A1 was of a similar appearance to the A2, but had a shorter wheelbase and a payload of only 30cwt. Both models were used by the retail trade and by many companies involved in the collection and delivery of parcels.

This model was seen at the Thornycroft Rally outside the company's old Basingstoke works in June 1991. Eric Sawford

1949 Thornycroft Sturdy Lorry

First produced in 1936 the Sturdy was designed for a 4ton payload and was available in three different wheelbase lengths. Initially the type was fitted with a 24hp four-cylinder petrol engine, but from 1945 a six-cylinder 30.6hp diesel engine was also available. A later option was a Meadows diesel engine. The Sturdy was used by many operators and seems to have been favoured by many brewery concerns. It remained in production until 1949 when it was replaced by the Sturdy Star. This was an improved version with a modern cab design. P. Chancellor

1956 Thornycroft Nippy Star Recovery Vehicle

The Thornycroft Nippy forward-control chassis was first produced in 1938 for a payload of three tons and continued to be available during the war years for those with the necessary licences for urgent war work. It was redesigned in 1951 and called the Nippy Star and the payload was increased to 4¹/2ton. It was available with either a Thornycroft 68bhp four-cylinder petrol engine or a Thornycroft 61bhp six-cylinder diesel engine. Later other engine options were also available. The Nippy Star ceased production in 1956, but not before the cabs had been changed to those made by an outside contractor. The replacement cabs were the same as those fitted to contemporary Guy vehicles.

This recovery vehicle started life as a tractor unit with Petter Engines, but was rebuilt as a recovery vehicle after having been written off following a serious accident. It is shown here at the Basingstoke Festival of Transport in May 1993. Peter Durham

1947 Vulcan 6PF Lorry

This design of Vulcan was introduced in 1939 after the firm had been taken over by Tilling Stevens and moved from Southport, Lancashire, to Maidstone in Kent. It was a well-designed, robust and reliable vehicle for a 6ton payload and was one of the few vehicles which could be manufactured for essential

civilian use during the war, providing that the purchaser had the necessary permit from the Ministry of War Transport. It was available with a four-cylinder petrol engine of 25.8hp (model 6FV) or a six-cylinder diesel engine of 29.4hp produced by Perkins (model 6PF).

This example, with standard 13ft wheelbase, was

originally owned by Nordic Steel Co Ltd. It ended its working life with a farmer in Worcestershire and is pictured here at South Shields in June 1993.
D. A. Reed

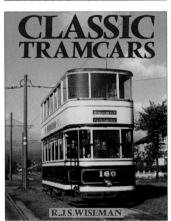